A Wild Onion Dinner

by Celeste Keys

Illustrated by Fabricio Vanden Broeck

Editorial Offices: Glenview, Illinois • Parsippany, New Jersey • New York, New York
Sales Offices: Needham, Massachusetts • Duluth, Georgia • Glenview, Illinois
Coppell, Texas • Sacramento, California • Mesa, Arizona

David was leaving school.
"David!" He heard his friend Marco's voice. "Do you want to come and play baseball with me?" Marco asked. "You can borrow my new baseball glove."

"Maybe later," said David. "Right now I have to go and dig wild onions with my mom. You and your mom can come too."

The two boys and their mothers went to look for wild onions. They went to a creek.

David's mother said, "We can find wild onions along the bank and in the shade."

David's mom showed them how to tell which plants were wild onions. She showed them how to dig up the onions with a stick.

"What are you going to do with all these wild onions?" Marco asked.

"We will have a Wild Onion Dinner," said David. "Do you want to come?"

"What is a Wild Onion Dinner?" Marco asked.

"It's a Muscogee tradition," said David. "My grandmother says that no one can be ready for summer until they have eaten wild onions in the spring."

Did You Know? About the Muscogee

- The Muscogee are a group of Native Americans.
- Sometimes the Muscogee people are called the Creeks, or the Creek people.

In this story, David and his mother are part of a Muscogee family.

"I want to be ready for summer!" said Marco. "I'll eat some wild onions. Are there other things to eat, too?"

"Sure," said David. "There will even be dessert."

"Will it be made of wild onions?" asked Marco.

David laughed and said no.

The next day, David and his mom gave a ride to Marco and Marco's mom. In the car they rode to the Wild Onion Dinner.

"Look at all the people!" said Marco. "The food must be really good."

"It is!" said David. "This is one dinner we don't want to miss. We have to get ready for summer and baseball, don't we?